The Book on LinkedIn®

How to Optimize Your Profile and More from a Recruiter's Perspective.

Nathanael Young MSHRM, CPRP, CRP

Copyright © 2025 by Nathanael Young

For permission requests, write to the publisher at:
Nathanaelyoung12@outlook.com

This book is a work of non-fiction. Names, characters, places, and incidents are either the products of the author's imagination or are used fictitiously. Any resemblance to actual people, living or dead, or actual events is entirely coincidental.

Library of Congress Cataloging-in-Publication Data
ISBN: 979-8-9940968-0-2
Cover design by H. Khan

Printed in the United States of America

LinkedIn is the registered trademark of LinkedIn Corporation or its affiliates. The use of the LinkedIn trademark in connection with this product does not signify any affiliation with or endorsement by LinkedIn Corporation or its affiliates.

PREFACE

In today's digital world, your LinkedIn profile is more than just an online resume; it is your professional brand and a gateway to countless opportunities. Whether you are actively seeking a new role, networking within your industry, or proving credibility in your field, a well-crafted LinkedIn profile can open doors and elevate your career. I authored this book to guide you through optimizing your profile through the eyes of a recruiter.

From capturing attention with a powerful headline to highlighting your skills and experiences, you will learn strategies to highlight your strengths and tell your professional story effectively. As you turn these pages, you will discover practical tips from a recruiter's perspective, insights to help you optimize your profile, expand your network, and use LinkedIn's features to achieve your goals.

How to use this book

Let me start by saying that you absolutely DO NOT have to read this book from front to back. I designed it to follow the natural flow of a LinkedIn user profile. So, if you are confident that you have already mastered the content of a particular chapter, feel free to skip and focus on the chapters that interest you most. In each chapter, I will share the recruiter's perspective on what we look for in that section, explain why it matters, and provide examples of what it should or should not look like.

DISCLOSURE

This book was written and conceptualized by Nathanael Young. I have utilized AI for editing and proofreading to ensure the highest quality of content while maintaining the integrity of my original ideas and voice.

ABOUT THE AUTHOR

My name is Nathanael Young. At the time of authoring this book, I am a Senior HR Recruiter for Leidos QTC Health Services and have been a user of LinkedIn since December 2017. I began my LinkedIn journey while serving as a Corpsman in the U.S. Navy; at the time, I was preparing for a potential transition out of the service. My presence on the platform was minimal, with around fifty connections; the majority of my profile sections were empty, and I never posted on it. To no one's surprise, I received exactly zero traction on the platform. In the end, I decided that reenlisting was in my best interest, and like most job seekers, I shelved my profile for a later day.

That day came on April 24, 2022, the day my daughter was born, and right there in the delivery room, I made the decision that I was not going to miss her childhood. I knew I would have to leave the military to be able to accomplish that humble goal. My service contract was set to end in November of that year unless I signed on for another re-enlistment. This gave me roughly six months to transition from an eight-year career and step into an entirely new world.

Through research and observation, I knew many who had successfully made career pivots found opportunities through LinkedIn. Therefore, like most job seekers, I dusted off my profile that I had not touched in years and started strategizing on how to land my next role. I started by taking advantage of LinkedIn's phenomenal offer to military service members by upgrading my profile to premium. Next, I began connecting with every single one of my phone contacts, colleagues, classmates, and friends. After that, I focused exclusively on talent acquisition specialists, industry leaders, and fellow military medicine professionals. I knew that LinkedIn gave around 75-100 free connection requests weekly, and I was going to make the most of them through personalized connection invites.

Did everyone respond? No, but the ones that did helped me build my network to 500 connections in my first month directly led to 12 job interviews. Of those 12, I got offers from 8 of them, including one that was my break into the recruitment field in the form of a 3-month skill bridge internship as a clinician recruiter for Pediatric Associates. Fast-forward a little over three years, and thanks to LinkedIn, I have been fortunate enough not only to make a successful transition into civilian life but also to carve out a new career path in recruitment.

This journey, both professionally and personally, has provided me with invaluable insights into how to use LinkedIn effectively. It has helped me land new roles, increase my base salary by 50% in 14 months, and grow in my career while also developing professionally. Today, I serve on the Human Resources Management Industry Advisory Council at American Military University, have mentored hundreds of job seekers on LinkedIn strategies, and delivered presentations on LinkedIn to universities, veteran organizations, and Fortune 500 companies eager to help their staff build strong professional brands on the platform. I hold a Master of Science in Human Resource Management from Western Governors University and hold multiple industry-leading certifications in Physician/Provider, tech, and corporate recruitment.

My goal with this book is to share the knowledge I have acquired through my own LinkedIn journey as well as through my professional role as a senior recruiter to help professionals at all experience levels optimize their LinkedIn experience.

TABLE OF CONTENTS

- Preface
- About the Author
- Chapter 1: Introduction to LinkedIn
- Chapter 2: Misconceptions
- Chapter 3: Profile Pictures, Cover Image, & Headlines
- Chapter 4: About Section
- Chapter 5: Activity Section
- Chapter 6: Experience Section
- Chapter 7: Education Section
- Chapter 8: License & Certifications Section
- Chapter 9: Volunteering Section
- Chapter 10 Skills & Endorsements Section
- Chapter 11: Recommendations Sections
- Chapter 12: Honors & Awards Section
- Chapter 13: Optional Sections
- Chapter 14: How to Actually Utilize LinkedIn
- Chapter 15: Messaging Do's & Don'ts
- Chapter 16: Joining LinkedIn Groups
- Chapter 17: Using LinkedIn Key Features
- Chapter 18: How to Spot Fake Profiles & Job Scams
- Chapter 19: Building Your Network with an Omni-Channel Approach
- Chapter 20: LinkedIn Learning
- Chapter 21: LinkedIn Premium
- Chapter 22: LinkedIn Recruiter
- Chapter 23: Final Thoughts
- Bibliography

CHAPTER 1

INTRODUCTION TO LINKEDIN

To better use LinkedIn, you first need to gain a better understanding of the platform itself.

TIMELINE OF LINKEDIN RELEVANT FOR JOBSEEKERS

Year	Milestone	Key Achievement
2002	The Concept	Founded by Reid Hoffman and team to digitize professional networks.
2003	The Launch	Official launch with a mission to connect the world's professionals.
2004	Early Scale	Surpassed **1 Million users**, proving the platform's viability.
2016	Strategic Exit	Acquired by **Microsoft for $26.2 Billion**, a tech industry landmark.
2023	Global Scale	Hit **1 Billion members** and launched **AI-driven** premium features.
2025	B2B Leader	Established as the **world's #1 site** for B2B marketing and sales.

LINKEDIN COMPANY VISION

"Create economic opportunity for every member of the global workforce."

LinkedIn Company Mission

"The mission of LinkedIn is simple: connect the world's professionals to make them more productive and successful."

LinkedIn has become the go-to social media platform for professionals aiming to connect with others in their industry. It is also the largest site in the world that is specifically for business-to-business marketing, business-to-client marketing, job searching, and recruitment.

NOTABLE LINKEDIN DEMOGRAPHICS

1. Total User Base:

- **Value:** 1.1 billion+ users (as of early 2025)

2. Age Distribution (Approximate Percentages):

Age Group	Percentage
25-34	50%
18-24	20%
35-54	20%
55+	5%
Unspecified	5%

3. Gender Distribution (Approximate Percentages):

Gender	Percentage
Male	57%
Female	43%

4. Top Geographical Markets (Millions of Users):

Region/Country	Users (Millions)
Asia-Pacific	343
North America	266
United States	239
Europe	314
India	155
Latin America	196
Brazil	83

5. Income & Education (U.S. Users - Approximate Percentages):

Category	Percentage
Earnings were $100K+	54%
Bachelor's Degree+	50%+
Master's Degree+	18%

HOW LINKEDIN WORKS

LinkedIn enables professionals and organizations to build profiles for connecting globally, promoting their business or services, sharing industry insights and ideas, and advancing their careers through mentorship and LinkedIn Learning.

Connections:

First Degree Connections:
These are individuals you are directly connected to because you have accepted their invitation, or they have received yours. They typically make up your immediate network, such as friends, colleagues, classmates, or professional contacts you know personally or through work. You can message them directly and view their complete profiles.

Second Degree Connections:
These people are linked to your first-degree contacts but not to you directly. Think of them as friends of a friend. You can view their profiles and may request to connect or be introduced through your mutual contacts, but can not message them directly without an InMail.

Third Degree Connections:
These individuals are connected to your second-degree contacts but not linked to you or your immediate connections. They are a bit more distant, but using LinkedIn's features like InMail or mutual introductions, you can potentially connect or reach out to them.

Professional Network:

Together, these degrees of connections form your professional network, and to expand it, you must connect with more individuals. There will be profiles that you are unable to view unless you have some cross-over in professional networks, be it either as a second or third degree connection. This professional network is critical for your success on the platform, so be strategic with whom you are allowing to be a part of it.

When it comes to your network, I want you to think of it as your garden because, in a way, what you sow is what you will reap. If you allow weeds to gather, then you will have a garden that takes and never produces. This could be in the form of connecting with "low value" profiles, such as individuals with six connections and no activity in the last 90 days, or individuals from countries with which you have no relationship. On the other hand, if you attend to your garden diligently by cultivating the right network, watering it with attention, and pruning it when necessary, you will reap a bountiful harvest. Similarly, to gardening, there are a lot of misconceptions that this next chapter will go over in depth.

CHAPTER 2

MISCONCEPTIONS

LinkedIn, like many digital platforms, is subject to numerous misconceptions. Here are some of the most common ones I've come across, and my recruiter answers them.

Misconception:
"Only job seekers need LinkedIn."

Fact:
No matter your employment status, LinkedIn is a valuable platform for networking, personal branding, business development, and professional growth. It is also widely used for B2B marketing, business-to-client outreach, and recruitment efforts.

Misconception:
"Creating a profile is all you need to attract opportunities automatically."

Fact:
While having a profile is a good starting point, ongoing effort is essential for success on LinkedIn. This includes actively networking, sharing quality content, and engaging with others. A well-crafted profile that highlights your strengths and captivates viewers can significantly enhance your presence and opportunities on the platform. Still, it's your activity that draws the most attention to your profile.

Misconception:

"Connecting with everyone is the key to success."

Fact:

Building your presence on LinkedIn is about balancing quality and quantity in your connections. Quality connections lead to meaningful engagement, professional opportunities, and knowledge sharing, while a larger network increases your visibility on the platform. Both are essential for growing your influence on the platform. It's all about what your goal is on the platform.

Misconception:

"LinkedIn is only beneficial for large corporations and recruiters."

Fact:

Small business owners, freelancers, students, and entrepreneurs also gain significant advantages from LinkedIn for networking, marketing, and building their professional brand.

Misconception:

"You need to be active every day to see results."

Fact:

Consistent activity is beneficial, but it does not have to be daily! Focusing on weekly, strategic, and targeted engagements such as commenting, liking posts, and occasionally sharing relevant content can be much more effective than random daily activity. LinkedIn even offers a "Weekly Sharing Tracker" to encourage members to comment, share, and create posts weekly.

Misconception:

"LinkedIn is just a digital resume."

Fact:

This is one of the most common misconceptions I hear. First, LinkedIn can be far more extensive as a professional autobiography than a resume ever could be. Second, it is much more than that; it is a social media platform for building your personal brand, sharing insights, engaging in discussions, and highlighting your expertise.

Misconception:

"I need to tailor my LinkedIn for the Applicant Tracking System (ATS)."

Fact:

This is a myth that job coaches, resume writers, and others who have never touched an ATS keep parroting for the last few years on the platform. Here is the real scoop: The ATS, for the most part, is a glorified electronic filing cabinet. It does precisely what is in the name, which is to track applicants throughout the entire hiring process. In that, every ATS is the same in the sense that it stores your application, resume, and other requested documents into a candidate profile. If you are hired, then that profile becomes the basis for your company personnel file. Now, where various ATS differ is in the bells and whistles that companies can elect to have included in their package, including candidate communication through email capability, candidate rating scores, connection with CRM, and various other features. I don't know of any of my recruiters in my 29,000+ followers on LinkedIn who are using any ATS/AI feature to scan LinkedIn profiles. Instead, it is always a set of human eyeballs that are quickly scanning your profile.

Recruiters use the ATS to post jobs on their company's career page and various other job boards, track candidate progress throughout the hiring process, and pull data, such as time to fill, for performance review. Understand, there is no magic format to make your LinkedIn profile, or your resume for that matter, "ATS" compliant. That is someone selling snake oil to you.

Misconception:
"The green banner makes you look desperate."

Fact:
As a recruiter, I have never heard any hiring manager or recruiter think the green banner signals desperation. In fact, we see it as a positive indicator that someone is actively open to opportunities, increasing the chances they will consider our role. Typically, only job coaches, resume writers, or content creators without HR or recruiting experience suggest otherwise, and that is because they stand to benefit from you seeking their services.

Honestly, I could author an entire book on this topic...and maybe I will someday. However, for now, this chapter covers the most common misconceptions about LinkedIn more than adequately. Feel free to send me your questions anytime on LinkedIn, and I will do my best to dispel any of the multitude of myths, misconceptions, and "best practices" floating around on the platform.

CHAPTER 3

PROFILE PICTURES, COVER IMAGE, & HEADLINES

Starting from the top of your profile, we will be discussing profile pictures, cover images, and headlines in this chapter. While it may seem irrelevant, having a professional profile picture is critical to your success on LinkedIn. From multiple studies, we know that having a profile photo results in up to 21x more profile views, 9x more connection requests, and a 36x increase in messages. All this equals more potential clients or job opportunities for you.

Recruiter Perspective

Below is a picture of what we see as recruiters when we are sourcing candidates via the search feature on LinkedIn.

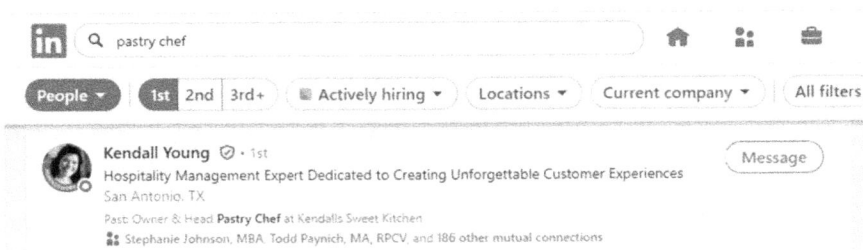

A strong photo and headline encourage me to view your profile as a recruiter. Your cover picture is the first thing I see beyond your profile picture and headline when I click on your profile.

This makes it prime real estate to show your passions, creativity, and personality.

PROFILE PICTURES

Your profile picture should be a professional headshot of you in professional attire that illustrates you as confident and professional. Keep the beach, party, or pictures with multiple people in them for Facebook. It is highly recommended that you smile and look approachable rather than have a scowl or look constipated. This is most people's first impression of you, so you want it to be a good one.

"What should I wear in my picture?"

Men- Wear a suit, button down, or polo with your hair brushed and beard trimmed.

Women- Wear a conservative blouse, button-down, or any outfit you would be comfortable wearing to the office. Avoid distracting makeup and keep hair brushed or put up.

Transitioning Service members and veterans: Dress for the job you want, not the one you have or previously held. You are coming into the civilian world, so you want to look the part.

Pro Tip
You do not have to pay $$$ for a professional headshot. Dress in professional attire and stand against a plain wall at home, or use a colored cloth or sheet as an alternative background. For professional attire, you can check out most major retailers or thrift stores like Goodwill. My first professional wardrobe was made up of name-brand suits like Hugo Boss, Joseph A. Banks, etc. that cost $13 from Goodwill, $40 for the tailoring, and around $10 for dry cleaning. Boom, now I had multiple suits that if I had purchased new would have easily cost me $500+ or

around $600 apiece. Also, consider using professional photo-editing software to ensure your headshot is polished and clear. Fantastic opportunity to explore various AI image generators to take an existing picture and create an ultra-realistic professional headshot.

Once you have your profile picture set up, you are given three options for picture banners: a green "Open to Work", a purple "Hiring", or no banner. As addressed in Chapter 2: Misconceptions, the green banner does not make you look desperate. In fact, it is there to highlight to the job market that you are available and open to new opportunities.

Recruiter Perspective: I have never looked at a profile with a green banner and said, "eww, they are desperate," nor have I heard similar from my recruiting colleagues, quite the opposite. We love it when we are sourcing and see a strong potential candidate with a green banner active. It allows us to message you for free without using an InMail credit, even if we are not directly connected. Anyone who tells you the green banner is desperate is either ignorant or trying to sell you something. If you can, turn the green banner to "public" instead of just "recruiters". The reason for this is that only recruiters who are paying for the top dollar package of LinkedIn Recruiter (around $10k a year for most companies) will be able to see that you are available to work, not every recruiter on LinkedIn. Again, the name of the game as a job seeker is VISIBILITY.

COVER IMAGE

This is the grey rectangle behind your profile picture. This is a prime marketing space to highlight your top valuable industry skills, professional branding statement, image of profession, or the services that you offer.

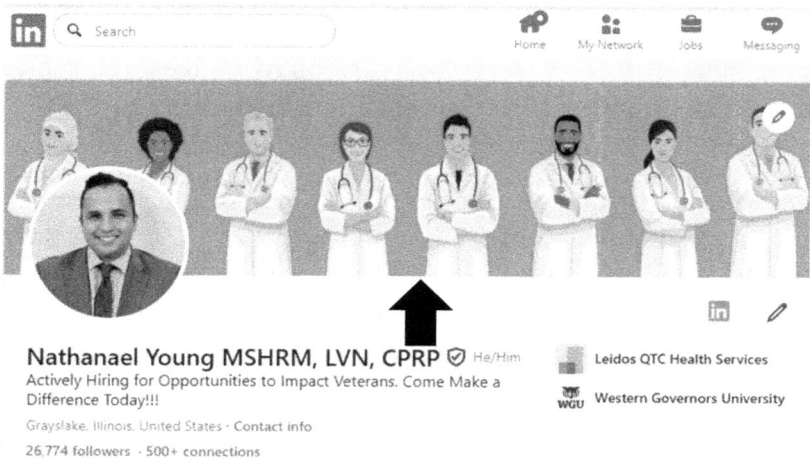

Nathanael Young MSHRM, LVN, CPRP ✓ He/Him
Actively Hiring for Opportunities to Impact Veterans. Come Make a
Difference Today!!!
Grayslake, Illinois, United States · Contact info
26,774 followers · 500+ connections

Leidos QTC Health Services

Western Governors University

Recruiter Perspective- My primary focus in my current role is clinician recruitment, hence why my cover picture is of a group of diverse clinicians, as they are my target audience. If I were a job seeker, I would use an image that captures who I am and what I bring to the table. This is an area where you can genuinely illustrate your creativity. A blank gray space is a missed opportunity to add some personality to your profile.

Pro Tip:
Use an AI image generator, a graphic design professional, or sites like Canva to help you design one that illustrates you best.

HEADLINE

This is the line right beneath your profile picture that is visible in searches and when viewing your profile. It is the most valuable 220 characters on your profile, and I want you to think of it as a professional brand/Elevator statement that can be in the form of an attention grabber or mission statement.

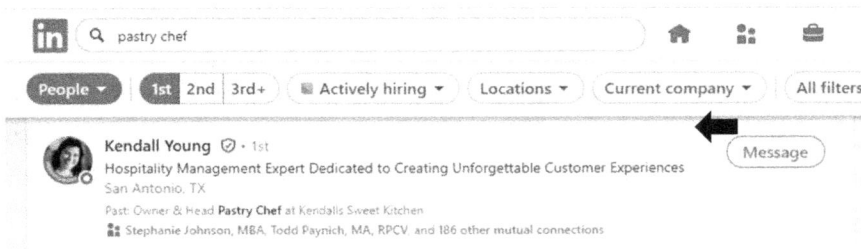

What not to have:
- Just your current job title and company.

- Nothing.

- Overused buzz words or phrases like "servant leader", "team player", "your next rockstar", or "transitioning service member."

- Vague text that contributes no value to your page or professional brand.

- Information that can easily be found in a profile, such as that you are a veteran, have an MBA, current organization, and so forth.

What you should have:

Jobseeker Example 1: "Full Stack Software Engineer | Built Mission Critical Cloud and Distributed Applications serving Government & Public Sectors | JavaScript, C# .NET, Java Spring, PostgreSQL, Oracle, MongoDB" **Reasoning-** Goes past just listing their current role. They also list what they did for what sector, and the languages/software they are familiar with that are relevant to their industry.

Jobseeker Example 2: "Talent Acquisition Expert | 172 Hires in 3 years | Specializing in Staffing Clinicians, Corporate, Tech, & Executive Roles | Passionate About Streamlining Recruitment & Building Creative Sourcing Strategies" **Reasoning-** Again states current role but further expands on it. It lists the field that they specialize in, quantifiable data that is attractive for the field, what specialties they recruit for, and what they are passionate about professionally.

Jobseeker Example 3: "Healthcare Operations Director | Oversee Daily Operations for High-Volume Primary Care Clinic with 12 clinicians | Managed $1M Budget & $2.2M in assets" Reasoning- Says their current role highlights quantifiable numbers that easily illustrate their scope and is a clear value proposition for any operations-related role.

Pro Tip:
Upload your resume bullets and job title into ChatGPT/AI engine with the prompt, "Create Headline for LinkedIn profile with keywords of your professional title, field, and a key quantifiable number from your experience section." Make sure to double-check for spelling and voice.

CHAPTER 4

ABOUT SECTION

The "About" section on LinkedIn is where you are given 2600 characters to introduce yourself to your audience, highlight your professional background, skills, achievements, career goals, what differentiates you from others in your industry/role, and a real opportunity to humanize yourself.

Recruiter Perspective

As a recruiter, I approach the "About" section like the dreaded "tell me about yourself?" interview question. You want it to offer ADDITIONAL insight into who you are, not just be a summary or rehash of everything listed on your LinkedIn profile. It is there to introduce John Smith, Amy Rodriguez, etc, to the world and the viewers of your page, a majority of whom have never met you. Share information that you are comfortable with a potential employer, coworker, or client knowing. I highly recommend avoiding political statements, identifying religion, possible health conditions, or anything else that could be inflammatory or could, unfortunately, open you up to potential discrimination.

Good Example

About

I am an accomplished hospitality management professional with a strong commitment to delivering unforgettable experiences for both clients and employees. My passion for management drives me to foster positive environments where team members can thrive while ensuring that client needs are met with the highest level of service.

Throughout my career, I have focused on balancing the demands of the workforce with those of the clientele, creating a harmonious atmosphere that promotes productivity, satisfaction, and loyalty. This foundational experience allowed me to successfully transition into the recruitment space, where I leverage my expertise in understanding organizational dynamics and talent needs.

I am dedicated to making a meaningful difference in the lives of candidates and the organizations I partner with, and I am eager to bring my background in hospitality management and recruitment to your team. Let's connect and explore how I can contribute to your organization's success!

Recruiter perspective

She discusses who she is and what she brings to the table. You can be as personable or as professional as you like. She used this section to highlight her experience in hospitality management before discussing her transition into the recruitment space. Tell us who YOU are. What drives you, what are you enthusiastic about, and maybe a fun fact or two. When I was looking for my first role post-service, I included a fun fact about myself at the bottom of my profile, which was that I raised chickens in my backyard. You'd be surprised how many individuals reached out using the chickens as a conversation starter, and sometimes it really was because they were genuinely interested in hearing more about raising chickens in a backyard. It caught their attention and opened the door for more conversations, which is exactly what we want the About section to do.

CHAPTER 5

ACTIVITY SECTION

The Activity section of a profile is where you can see a user's previous posts, comments, images, videos, articles, newsletters, events, and documents. Probably one of the most underutilized sections on a majority of job seekers' profiles. As a recruiter, I always call this the "Peacock" section because it is really what draws attention to your profile and is massively influential in helping you build a significant and engaging presence on the platform. Creating content significantly enhances your profile's visibility.

Many job seekers report challenges with this section; the three concerns listed below are commonly named during mentoring sessions.

- **Impostor syndrome-** "A psychological condition that is characterized by persistent doubt concerning one's abilities or accomplishments accompanied by the fear of being exposed as a fraud despite evidence of one's ongoing success" (Merriam-Webster's Dictionary).

- **Lack of creativity/inspiration-** I would say about 80% of job seekers I have mentored or spoken with have said this is one of the greatest reasons. Often saying, "What would I even post about?"

- **Unclear goals**: Not specifying whether content is meant to increase profile traffic, raise awareness, or build subject matter authority.

Below is how you overcome these common issues.

- Own your craft. You chose your profession, and you do it daily...own it. If you lack the confidence to do so, then you either need to work on improving it through mentorship, knowledge seeking with seminars, research, diversifying your professional experience, or leave the field altogether because you are not going to succeed in it long term.

    My story: When I first broke into the recruitment field, I suffered from all three of these. To overcome them, I buckled down and studied as much information as I could through joining professional social media groups via LinkedIn to hear what recruiters were talking about, what their gripes were, new emerging technology, and industry knowledge. I got my first break in the recruitment field through a 3-month internship that then transitioned into a full-time role. I volunteered for everything I could, asked questions, and found experienced mentors who helped guide me throughout my journey.

- Start with what you know and then be comfortable exploring new media. I first started with posting memes before writing short-form posts, then long-form articles, and recently graduated to the latest, which is videos. Right now, 2025, we are seeing a massive push from LinkedIn's marketing team and the LinkedIn algorithm to encourage more videos. The algorithm currently favors video content because it provides more engaging content that users are familiar with via other platforms like TikTok, Facebook Reels, and YouTube Shorts. All social media platforms want content that keeps users engaged, is relevant to modern trends, and inspires others to follow.

Pro-tip: Use AI generation engines to aid you with brainstorming and editing your content.

- Sit down and strategize what exactly you intend to achieve with posting on LinkedIn. Are you aiming to expand your audience, increase brand visibility, prove expertise, present accomplishments, or raise awareness? Once you have that, then you can really start strategizing what your initial approach to content creation will be. Understand that this will shift with the ebb and flows of the LinkedIn algorithm, as well as from yourself as you become more confident in putting yourself out there.

TYPES OF CONTENT/ACTIVITY

1. **TEXT:** The most common form of content is text. You can write varying-length posts that can be calls to action, highlights of recent achievements, or share an opinion on professional topics.

Repeat after me:

Remote is a work location, not a job. Remote is a work location, not a job. Remote is a work location, not a job... Let's say this 50 more times.

Please stop messaging me about "remote work" in a way that doesn't help either of us. Instead, I'd appreciate if you could reach out with something like this:

"Hi Nathanael, (just a quick note—please spell my name correctly; it's Nathanael, not Nathaniel). I've explored your organization's job board and have applied for the following role: [insert job title/req number]. Could you share insights about the organization, such as benefits, culture, and the hiring process?"

If we don't currently have the ideal role for you, consider reaching out with:

"Hi Nathanael, I'm an experienced [insert your profession] looking for my next opportunity. I've reviewed your job board and noticed there aren't any openings that align with my skills right now. Do you know of any upcoming roles that align with that field or know anyone who may have one?"

Let's make our conversations more productive.

#recruiterinsights #LinkedInmessages #thisnotthat

🅒🅔🅞 388   56 comments · 11 reposts

2. **Polls:** Polls are where you ask your audience their opinion on the matter and provide them with limited options to select from. These are fantastic for conducting market research and gauging your audience's opinion on relevant   topics.

   Influencer Tip- Polls can help significantly increase your impressions and post engagement as they encourage users to share their opinions. Utilizing the "celebrate occasion" to speak on a recent achievement, such as certification, work milestone, or promotion, tends to perform very well on the algorithm and garner a large amount of engagement.

Nathanael Young MSHRM, LVN, CPRP 🔗 · You
Actively Hiring for Opportunities to Impact Veterans. Come Make a Difference...
Visit my website
8mo · 🌐

Reason I ask this is because I just had a candidate that was very upset for receiving a rejection call yesterday because it was two days before Christmas....Hence this short poll. I am genuinely curious how yall feel on the subject. As a recruiter, I reject/decline as they come during the process without regards of holidays because not everyone celebrates them and I want to be quick in my communication. I never want candidates to delay or outright miss another opportunity waiting for our response. As a candidate I would feel the same way.

So what are your thoughts?

#poll #question #insights #holidays #opinions

When is the best time to reject/decline candidate during holiday season?

You can see how people vote. Learn more

Before	38%
After	49%
During	13%

387 votes · Poll closed

3. **COMMENTS:** Every time you comment on another user's post, people viewing your profile will be able to see that in your activity section, so be mindful, don't be a troll, or get into intense arguments that could reflect poorly on you to outside viewers.

All activity

(Posts) (**Comments**) (Videos) (Images) (More ▾)

Nathanael Young MSHRM, LVN, CPRP commented on this   · · ·

4. **IMAGES:** Pretty straightforward, as this is where you post an image, such as a meme, flyer, or picture, and can post it either alone or with text above. I found memes to be a great disruptor from the doom and gloom we often see on LinkedIn, and they do well on both engagement and impressions.

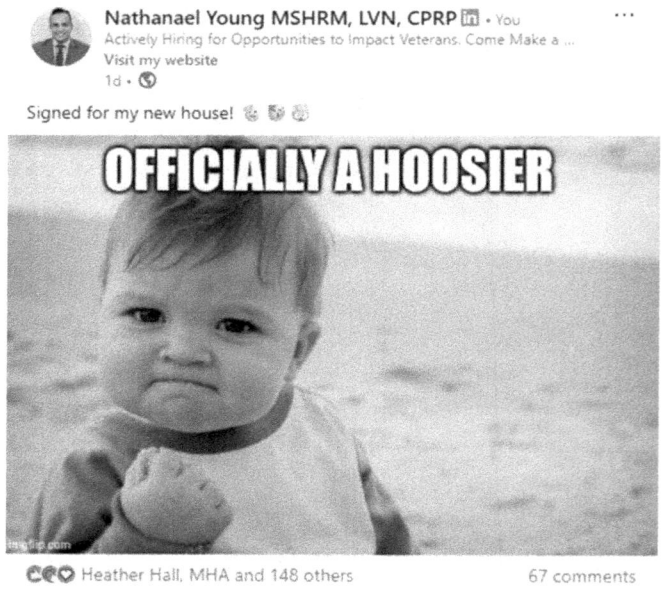

5. **VIDEOS:** The newest addition to LinkedIn content is currently receiving the most love from the algorithm. Make sure to review them before and after you post them to ensure you are putting out a product that accurately reflects you and your professional brand.

All activity

Posts | Comments | **Videos** | Images | More ▾

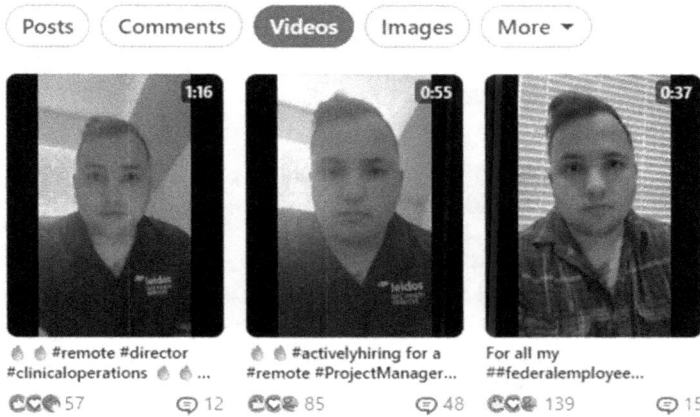

🔥 🔥 #remote #director
#clinicaloperations 🔥 🔥 ...
💬 57   💬 12

🔥 🔥 #activelyhiring for a
#remote #ProjectManager...
💬 85   💬 48

For all my
##federalemployee...
💬 139   💬 15

6. **ARTICLES:** Provides you with a much greater character count than your standard post, and is more formal appearing. Use this space to write in detail about topics you know well or feel enthusiastic about. If you title them with SEO in mind, then there is a higher likelihood that they will get picked up in searches off the platform, such as a Google or Bing search. This could be a great traffic generator for your page and engagement.

All activity

Posts   Comments   Videos   Images   **More ▾**

The Rise of AI and Decimation of the American White Collar...

Delaina Morse Corey Maywald, MBA, ACIR, CASR, CSMR, PRC Kendall Youn...

by Nathanael Young MSHRM, LVN, CPRP • 7 min read

Educational Pathways: The Advantages of Pursuing an...

Associate degrees have often been overlooked by society in favor of thei...

by Nathanael Young MSHRM, LVN, CPRP • 3 min read

"Unveiling the Hidden Value of Fast Food Jobs: A Personal...

7. **REPOSTING:** Sharing another user's post to show your support, amplify their message, or highlight content you find valuable. You are then given the option to either write your own post above the content or just post as is to your feed. I always recommend writing in addition to the post. You could share your own opinion, state why you agree with the original content creator, or why your audience should view the content you are sharing. Use Hashtags as well to help with SEO!

Nathanael Young MSHRM, LVN, CPRP reposted this   · · ·

●●●●●●●●●●●●●●●●●●● ✔ · 1st
Recruiter
6d · Edited · ⊙

Hi LinkedIn!

I'm currently looking for **1099 Ophthalmologists or Optometrists** to **support** the Reserve **Health Readiness Program (RHRP)** in the **Carson City. NV area.**

If you or someone in your network is interested in flexible contract work performing **Occupational Health / RHRP eye exams**, I'd love to connect.

Why This Opportunity Stands Out:
• One-time exams only — no treatment or follow-up required
• No insurance billing or VA invoicing — we pay you directly
• Prompt, guaranteed payments — issued twice monthly (8th & 22nd)
• Flexible scheduling — exams are conducted at your clinic
• Streamlined charting — online reporting with simple click-based documentation

These events help ensure our service members stay medically ready, and your support makes a real impact.

If you're interested or know a provider who might be, please message me

8. **DOCUMENTS:** This can include PowerPoints and documents that you share in posts. For example, the "Documents" tab in my Activity section holds a resume workshop PowerPoint, multiple resume templates, and other resources that I have uploaded to provide support for job seekers and followers.

All activity

Posts   Comments   Videos   Images   More ▾

FREE CV Template - 3 pages

First Name Last Name, MSN/PA/MD
City, State, Zip Code
Email: Randomemail@gmail.com | Phone: 1-800-867-5309 LinkedIn URL

EDUCATION

Degree	Field of Study	Institution, Location	Date
MSN/PA/MD	Family Nurse Practitioner	Random School, Location	Year-Year

LICENSURE, CERTIFICATION & TRAINING

Licensure	Certifying Body	Date
RN/PA/NP/MD 000000	State/nation board	Year
DEA 000000	State	Year

Certification & Training	Certifying Body	Date
Certified Family Nurse Practitioner	American Association of Nurse Practitioners	Year
Pediatric Advanced Life Support (PALS)	American Heart Association	Year
Advanced Cardiac Life Support (ACLS)	American Heart Association	Year
Basic Life Support (BLS)	American Heart Association	Year

RESEARCH INTEREST

• H

FNP/PA/MD/DO PRACTICUM EXPERIENCE

Utilize this checklist to help with your content creation on LinkedIn.

CONTENT CREATION CHECK LIST

1. Planning & Strategy

- **Define your goal-** Which will stem from four key areas, including awareness, generating leads, establishing your subject matter authority, or building your page's engagement. By identifying your goal, you will be able to begin developing a content campaign strategy.

- **Identify your target audience-** Who are you hoping to engage with? Are they senior leaders in your industry that you are planning to market your service or product to, your industry peers, or just a general audience to build traffic? The more specific you are, the more it will influence the type of content you will want to create.

- **Research trending topics and hashtags-** LinkedIn, like all social media platforms, wants its platform feeds to be active and trending with topics that their users will be interested in. A simple Google search of "trending topics on LinkedIn" will reveal what is currently trending on the platform. From there, curate your content to the trending topic to increase engagement. Hashtags are a fantastic tool for improving your content's discoverability and increasing your posts' visibility for users seeking those keywords.

- **Create a content calendar for consistent posting-** Inspiration finds us all at different times. Sometimes it's during lunch, and for others it's while they are in the shower. Whenever it is, LinkedIn allows you to create content and schedule it to be posted later.

2. Content Development

- Choose content type (image, text, video, infographic, carousel)

- Ensure content is relevant and provides value.

- Incorporate trending and evergreen topics that stay constantly relevant.

3. Creation & Optimization

- Use high-quality visuals and engaging videos.

- Write clear, concise, and compelling copy with a strong call to action.

- Thoroughly spell check and proofread.

- Add relevant hashtags and keywords for search engine optimization.

- Tag relevant individuals or organizations. This can increase your engagement and widen your visibility.

- Include links in the comments, not in the actual post. LinkedIn wants you to stay on its site, not be redirected to others.

4. Post-Upload Checks

- Preview your post to check layout and visuals.

- Ensure adherence to LinkedIn guidelines.

- Post when your audience is most active.

5. Post-Engagement

- Respond promptly to comments and messages.

- Encourage discussions with questions or prompts.

- Track performance with LinkedIn analytics.

- Refine your strategy based on insights.

6. Additional Tips

- Use authentic, personal voice.

- Maintain consistent branding and style.

- Reuse or update successful content.

CHAPTER 6

EXPERIENCE SECTION

The Experience section of your LinkedIn profile is one of the most crucial aspects of your profile because it shows your professional background and career history. It allows you to detail your earlier roles, responsibilities, achievements, and skills gained in each position. In this chapter, I will show examples of what not to do and provide advice on how to improve your current section.

First, the key components of the Experience section include the following,

- Company name
- Your tenure there, starting with the month and year.
- Location of the job
- Job title
- Description of your role there also includes quantifying the scope of your responsibilities and the impact of your achievements.
- Tagged Skills

EXAMPLE OF WHAT NOT TO DO IN YOUR EXPERIENCE SECTION

Example A – No job descriptions under your position.

← Experience   +

Leidos QTC Health Services
Full-time · 1 yr 7 mos
Remote
in helped me get this job

Strategic Sourcing Recruiter   ⌀
Feb 2025 - Present · 6 mos

Senior Human Resources Recruiter   ⌀
Jan 2024 - Feb 2025 · 1 yr 2 mos
San Antonio, Texas Metropolitan Area

Example B – Filling the experience section with your company's description.

Nathanael Young MSHRM, LVN, CPRP (He/Him)
Actively Hiring for Opportunities to Impact Veterans Lives

← Experience   +

Leidos QTC Health Services
Full-time · 1 yr 7 mos
Remote
in helped me get this job

Strategic Sourcing Recruiter   ⌀
Feb 2025 - Present · 6 mos

Leidos QTC Health Services collaborates closely with government and non-government customers to address current and future program needs within the health services domain. We specialize in disability-focused medical examinations, independent medical exams and review services, occupational health services, diagnostic testing and case management solutions. As innovators, we focus on advancing technologies that improve service delivery, with a particular emphasis on enhancing accessibility for examinees in rural communities. With a proven track record of continuous improvement and steady growth, we now handle over 2.8 million appointments annually.

Skills: Executive Search · Strategic Sourcing · Relationship Development · Passive Candidate Generation · Interviewing

Recruiter Perspective

It's a missed opportunity when job seekers have Experience sections that look like the examples above, just listing their job title without any additional details or filling the section with a description of the company they work for. This is the perfect opportunity to showcase their scope of responsibility and achievements. Think of it this way: 99% of the people viewing your profile have no idea who you are or what you do. We might have a general idea of what a recruiter or professional in your field does, but we don't know what YOU specifically did in that role. You have up to 2000 characters to describe your responsibilities and accomplishments, so make them count. Use that space to tell your story and highlight your value.

Unlike your resume, which is limited by space, your LinkedIn Experience section allows you to go much deeper. Use bullet points to clearly outline your responsibilities and achievements, and strive to quantify results whenever possible. Quantifying is the best way to illustrate your scope of responsibilities for the role as well as highlight your impact. Use AI tools like ChatGPT to improve your bullet points and boost SEO. This approach creates a keyword-rich profile that increases your chances of showing up in searches conducted by recruiters. Recruiters often use Boolean search strings, which use keywords to filter candidates. Therefore, including relevant keywords in your profile can help match you to potential opportunities. Be sure to tag industry-relevant and desirable skills that you showed in these roles. If a recruiter is using LinkedIn Recruiter, they can filter their search results based on these skills, increasing your chances of being discovered.

OPTIMIZED EXAMPLE OF THE EXPERIENCE SECTION,

Nathanael Young MSHRM, LVN, CPRP (He/Him)
Actively Hiring for Opportunities to Impact Veterans Lives

Leidos QTC Health Services
Full-time · 1 yr 7 mos
Remote
in helped me get this job

Strategic Sourcing Recruiter
Feb 2025 - Present · 6 mos

* Responsible for managing full-cycle recruitment process, including candidate sourcing, screening, interviewing, offer, negotiating, and hiring for candidates in various fields from clinical medicine (NP/PA/Audiologist), corporate roles (Project Management, IT, and Marketing), executive roles (Clinical Ops Director, Medical Directors, Chief Product Officer, and Director of Product Engineering).
* Serving as a trusted advisor to internal stakeholders to better understand talent acquisition needs, job qualifications, experience, and competencies, leading to more efficient candidate sourcing, but also providing strategic input on various aspects of the recruitment field.
* Created and executed highly effective proactive recruitment strategies to identify top talent for positions, ensuring internal client satisfaction.
* Participated in employer spotlight events, job fairs, recruiting events, podcasts, school interviews, and other company information sessions to help establish potential candidate pipelines and brand ambassadorship.
* Prioritized critical staffing areas by effectively managing 8-12 high-level reqs monthly.
* Hired a total of 15 clinicians and corporate staff for various full-time positions across the U.S., decreasing employee burnout while increasing potential revenue for the organization. Have had 3 W2 referrals hired throughout the organization in addition to another 15 1099 pending.

Skills: Executive Search · Strategic Sourcing · Relationship Development · Passive Candidate Generation · Interviewing

As you can see, I have added bullets and tagged relevant skills detailing both my responsibilities and accomplishments in my current role. This will increase the likelihood of me appearing in more searches because this section is now search engine optimized.

CHAPTER 7

EDUCATION SECTION

The Education section of your profile covers your educational journey, achievements, and relevant coursework. Its primary purpose is to highlight your academic education for potential employers, recruiters, and professional contacts. LinkedIn also uses this information to display your profile to other users in the "People you may know from [school name]" section on the "My Network" tab of your profile.

Recruiter Perspective

The majority of our roles require that you meet specific educational requirements, such as a bachelor's degree in business or a related field, or an associate degree in lab science. Having this listed on your LinkedIn allows us to verify that you meet the minimum requirements for the role we are sourcing for and increases the likelihood of us reaching out to you to discuss further.

Tips to improve this section,

1. List all the schools you have attended, as this will widen your network presentation.

2. List of your major

3. List your activities and societies (Societies are great networking opportunities for both students and alumni)

4. Provide a brief description of your program. I like to use the program description provided by the university.

Bad Example-

Nathanael Young MSHRM, LVN, CPRP (He/Him)
Actively Hiring for Opportunities to Impact Veterans Lives

← Education ◇ +

American Military University ✎

Purdue Global ✎

WGU Western Governors University ✎

Optimized Example-

Nathanael Young MSHRM, LVN, CPRP (He/Him)
Actively Hiring for Opportunities to Impact Veterans Lives

← Education ◇ +

WGU Western Governors University ✎
Master of Science - MS, Human Resource Management
Nov 2023 - Sep 2024
Grade: 3.0

The Master of Science in Human Resource Management is a competency-based, online, graduate degree program with industry-relevant coursework designed to align with both SHRM (Society for Human Resource Management) and HRCI (HR Certification Institute) curriculum content standards and guidelines. These standards and guidelines help students prepare for either the SHRM-CP or the HRCI PHR certification exams. This compact program contains 10 courses that combine general business competencies with core human resource (HR) management skills and has a unique capstone experience that embeds the SHRM Inclusive Workplace Culture specialty credential. Along the way to degree = completion, students will also earn a WGU certificate in HR Technology and Analytics for Decision Making. Throughout the program, themes of strategic HR decision-making and critical thinking, global HR best practices, and DEI are interspersed within the coursework.

American Military University ✎
Bachelor of Arts - BA, Business, Management, Marketing, and Related Support Services
Feb 2021 - Jun 2022
Grade: 3.78

Activities and societies: Salute, SCLA, SHRM, VP of Professional Development for SHRM

Graduated Magna Cum Laude

CHAPTER 8

LICENSE & CERTIFICATIONS SECTION

The "Licenses & Certifications" section of your LinkedIn profile is meant to display any official credentials, licenses, or certifications you've obtained. It enables you to showcase your specialized skills/knowledge that sets you apart from other candidates as well as aids in building instant credibility with employers, clients, or collaborators. Additionally, this section helps recruiters and employers find candidates with specific certifications that match their requirements.

Recruiter Perspective

This section is like your education section, as hiring managers often look for candidates with specific licenses or certifications. Listing them clearly and keeping them up to date is essential for appearing in more searches and increasing the likelihood of being approached by recruiters

What to include:

1. Name of credential

2. Issuing organization's name

3. Dates of issuance and expiration.

4. Be sure to tag relevant skills.

5. Credential ID & URL (if applicable)

Good Example-

Nathanael Young MSHRM, LVN, CPRP (He/Him)
Actively Hiring for Opportunities to Impact Veterans Lives

← **Licenses & certifications** +

Certified Physician/Provider Recruitment Professional ✎
Association for Advancing Physician and Provider Recruitment (AAPPR)
Issued Feb 2025 · Expires Feb 2028

(Show credential ☑)

Skills: healthcare recruitment · talent acquisition · Physician Recruitment · provider recruitment · clinician recruitment · Physician Network Development · Screening Resumes · Candidate Assessment · Passive Candidate Generation

American Staffing Association Corporate Recruiting Professional Certificate ✎
American Staffing Association
Issued Oct 2024

(Show credential ☑)

Skills: Job Description Development · Talent Management · Hiring

Recruiter Pro Tip - LinkedIn Learning and Coursera provide access to a plethora of certifications for an affordable monthly subscription. These platforms allow you to expand further your professional knowledge as well as increase your value proposition to potential employers.

CHAPTER 9

VOLUNTEERING SECTION

The "Volunteering" section on LinkedIn enables you to highlight your participation in volunteer activities and community service. Its key purpose is to highlight your dedication to giving back and reflecting your values beyond your professional experience. Additionally, it offers an opportunity to display competencies such as leadership, collaboration, project management, and empathy, all of which are pertinent to your professional development.

The key components of the "Volunteering" section match those of the "Experience" section, including:

- Organization name
- Volunteer role title
- Cause
- Tenure with the organization
- Description of your role there

Recruiter perspective

Volunteering is an excellent way to broaden your experience beyond your regular professional role and duties. For example, imagine you're a medical assistant aiming to advance into a lead medical assistant position but lack formal leadership experience; volunteering can fill that gap. For instance, let's say you are a team leader for a Red Cross disaster response team. By leading a

Red Cross disaster team, you are now gaining valuable professional experience in how to lead people and manage resources, which in turn allows you to increase your value proposition for your desired role. It's also a great gap filler for those unable to work a full-time job due to extenuating circumstances, like military spouses and stay-at-home parents.

Example of Volunteer section-

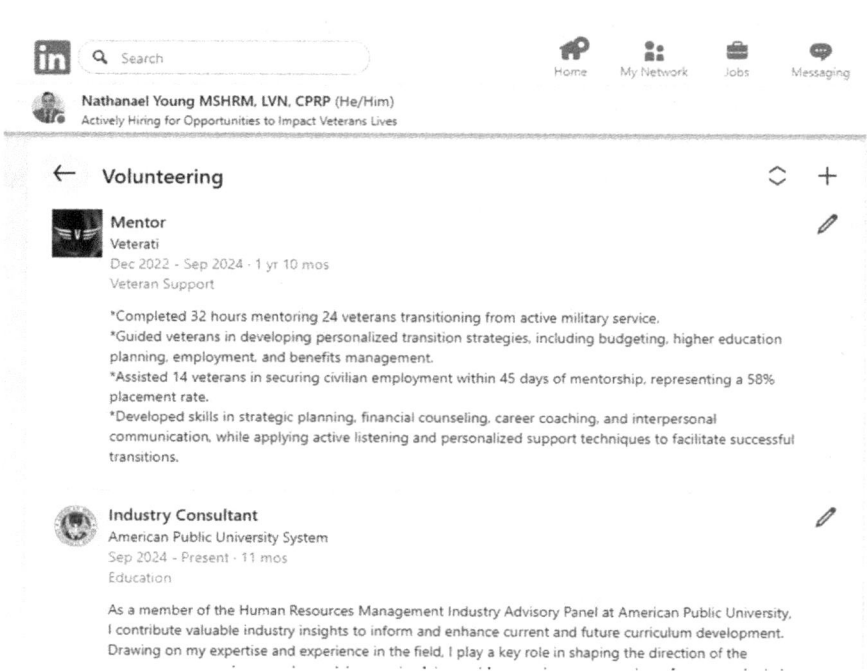

Pro Tip: Use prompt in AI generator "Rewrite the LinkedIn volunteer section, please include quantifiable achievements and key skills for each volunteer role. Highlight specific contributions with numbers or measurable results, and emphasize relevant skills demonstrated or developed in each position."

CHAPTER 10

SKILLS & ENDORSEMENTS SECTION

The Skills section on your LinkedIn profile is massively influential in increasing your profile's visibility and strengthening your brand. In today's competitive job market, it is one of the best ways to optimize your profile by enabling recruiters to find you through relevant keywords and skills searches. Refining this section boosts your visibility while at the same time highlighting your strengths and expertise.

You can tag up to 100 skills in your Experience, Education, License & Certification, or Skills section. So, choose wisely! Don't just list a bunch of random skills to fill out this section. Instead, be strategic by first researching the 100 most desirable skills in your industry or for your role, then select those that apply to you. After that, I would recommend tagging skills you currently have that could bleed over to higher-level or leadership roles.

To understand the importance of the Skills section, I want to illustrate to you how a recruiter sources their candidates on LinkedIn. Recruiters utilize either the advanced filters through LinkedIn Recruiter/Recruiter Lite or a Boolean search string to locate potential candidates more effectively. Boolean search strings rely on Boolean operators. "Boolean operators form the basis of mathematical sets and database logic.

- They connect your search words to either narrow or broaden your set of results.

- The three basic Boolean operators are: **AND, OR,** and **NOT**.

Why use Boolean operators?

- To focus on a search, particularly when your topic holds multiple search terms.

- To connect various pieces of information to find exactly what you're looking for." (*LibGuides: Database Search Tips: Boolean Operators*, n.d.)

- Example of Boolean Search String: "Project Manager" AND "PMP" AND "Healthcare" OR "Tech" NOT "Construction"

Recruiter perspective: As a recruiter who specializes in sourcing highly qualified candidates for hard-to-fill roles, Boolean Search Strings are my bread and butter. Adding industry-relevant, sought-after skills to your profiles makes it easier to appear in more searches. I like the idea of skill endorsements on LinkedIn, but unfortunately, I've seen this section abused the most on the platform, with strangers I've never met endorsing my skills they never witnessed. Another aspect of the standard skill endorsement is that it does not allow you to articulate specific examples of the skill being utilized. Alternatively, I suggest endorsing only those skills you have personally seen in the user's Recommendations section. It's the perfect opportunity to articulate your witnessing of the skills in action as well as their impact on them.

Example of skills in the Experience section-

Nathanael Young MSHRM, LVN, CPRP (He/Him)   Resources   Visit my web
Actively Hiring for Opportunities to Impact Veterans Lives

Experience   +   ✎

Leidos QTC Health Services
Full-time · 1 yr 7 mos
Remote
in helped me get this job

Strategic Sourcing Recruiter
Feb 2025 - Present · 6 mos

* Responsible for managing full-cycle recruitment process, including candidate sourcing, screening, interviewing,
offering, negotiating, and hiring for candidates in various fields from clinical medicine (NP/PA/Audiolc ...see more

♡ Presentation Skills, Social Media Management and +21 skills

Example of Skills in Education section-

Nathanael Young MSHRM, LVN, CPRP (He/Him)
Actively Hiring for Opportunities to Impact Veterans Lives

← Education   ↻   +

Western Governors University
WGU Master of Science - MS, Human Resource Management   ✎
Nov 2023 - Sep 2024

Grade: 3.0

The Master of Science in Human Resource Management is a competency-based, online, graduate degree
program with industry-relevant coursework designed to align with both SHRM (Society for Human
Resource Management) and HRCI (HR Certification Institute) curriculum content standards and guidelines.
These standards and guidelines help students prepare for either the SHRM-CP or the HRCI PHR certification
exams. This compact program contains 10 courses that combine general business competencies with core
human resource (HR) management skills and has a unique capstone experience that embeds the SHRM
Inclusive Workplace Culture specialty credential. Along the way to degree = completion, students will also
earn a WGU certificate in HR Technology and Analytics for Decision Making. Throughout the program,
themes of strategic HR decision-making and critical thinking, global HR best practices, and DEI are
interspersed within the coursework.

Skills: Human Resources (HR) · Organization Skills

Example of skills in the License & Certification section-

Example of skills in the Skills section-

Pro Tip: Use the prompt "Generate a comprehensive list of the top 100 skills essential for a (Position Title) working in the (blank) industry, including technical, leadership, communication, and industry-specific skills." To get a good start on the skills section of your profile, you can tag skills to specific sections as you see fit.

CHAPTER 11

RECOMMENDATIONS SECTIONS

The Recommendations section is there to help build credibility and enhance the user's professional reputation by providing third-party endorsements of their skills and work ethic. It allows profile viewers to gain insights beyond what's listed on your profile/resume by providing third-party validation. I want you to think of this section as akin to how online reviews work for organizations and products. You can invite your manager, coworkers, and previous clients to leave recommendations as a form of social proof of your superior performance and skills.

Recruiter Perspective

I absolutely read a profile's recommendation, especially for individuals potentially being hired for leadership roles. The catch, though, is that I look at the recommendations they've given more than the ones they've received. I want to see how they advocate for their team members. For individuals not in leadership positions, I read the recommendations to hear from their coworkers/ managers on how to work with them. Finally, when I'm reviewing someone's profile who offers services, I always look at the reviews to hear about other clients' experiences.

Tips for section: You can request and give recommendations, but only if you have a section set up on your profile and vice versa. If you ask for one, make sure to have them avoid generic praise and give specific examples of your skills and contributions. The same goes for the recommendations that you provide for others.

Example of a good recommendation-

The reason these two are good is that they are commenting on specific services that I provided them and their impact on them.

Example of a bad recommendation-

LinkedIn

🔍 I'm looking for...   Home   My Network   Jobs   Messaging

Nathanael Young MSHRM, LVN, CPRP (He/Him)
Join Us in Making a Difference for America's Heroes Today!

← **Recommendations**   +

Received   Given   Pending

Kendall Young `Received` · 1st   . . .
Hospitality Management Expert Dedicated to Creating Unforgettable Customer Experiences
December 1, 2025. Kendall reported directly to Nathanael

(Add to profile)

Nate is a good worker. He does his job.

This recommendation is vague, unenthusiastic, and lacks specific details about skills or accomplishments, making it ineffective for highlighting the person's strengths.

CHAPTER 12

HONORS & AWARDS SECTION

The Honors & Awards section on LinkedIn is a dedicated space designed to highlight your notable achievements and recognitions, allowing visitors to see your professional accolades. This section enables you to highlight a wide range of accomplishments, from industry awards and accolades to recognition received from professional organizations, educational institutions, or community groups.

Recruiter Perspectives

This is a great section to really show off the recognition you've received. Don't just say you are a top performer; instead, show it. A top performer spot award is a perfect illustration of this. Whenever possible, provide context for why you received the award.

What to Include:

- **Professional Awards:** Recognition won in your industry, such as "Best Salesperson of the Year," "Innovator Award," or "Top Performer."

- **Medals and Honors:** Military medals, service awards, or honors received for outstanding performance and dedication.

- **Academic or Institutional Honors:** Dean's list mentions, scholarships, fellowships, or special recognitions from universities and educational institutions.

- **Organizational Recognitions:** Honors from professional bodies or organizations, such as "Member of the Year," leadership awards, or lifetime achievements.

- **Community or Volunteer Awards:** Recognitions for community service, volunteering, or social impact initiatives.

Fill in details such as:

- Name of the award/honor
- Issuer or organization
- Date received
- Description or context (optional but recommended)
- URL
- Picture of Award

Tips for Optimization:
Be specific and provide context to help viewers understand the significance.

Honors & awards   + 🖉

Spot Award- For Social Media and Veteran Community Engagement
Issued by Leidos QTC Health Services · Mar 2025

Associated with Leidos QTC Health Services

Outstanding Award.pdf

Navy Achievement Medal
Issued by U.S. Navy · Nov 2022

Associated with US Navy

I've earned two Navy achievement medals during my time in the Navy for going above and beyond. My first one was for a two month rotation in Norway where I assisted the camps preventive medical officer in daily water tests, living   ...see more

My first corporate award was a "spot award" to recognize my brand ambassadorship on social media as well as my engagement with the veteran community. With my Navy achievement medal, I listed out the backstory for these awards. This allows me to provide more depth to awards that are unknown to most individuals who have not served in the U.S. Navy.

CHAPTER 13

OPTIONAL SECTIONS

This chapter is going to be my catch-all chapter for the remaining sections of the profile in the name of keeping this book from looking like a college textbook. With that, I will leave it to you, the individual reader, to decide if you wish to have them on your profile. These sections include Publications, Projects, Courses, Test Scores, Organizations, Causes, Patents, and Languages. Pretty straightforward. Going to go through each briefly.

Publications Section- Where you can list the books, published articles, and papers that you have authored. Include the URL to the documents for others to explore further if they are interested. For example, by the time you are reading this book, it will be listed in this section on my profile. This can be a critical area for those in academia or those who are freelance/professional writers.

Projects Section- This section is suitable for college students, interns, and individuals who are working on projects outside of their professional occupation. For example, I've seen individuals who are trying to break into the tech field list the various projects they have completed, or college students discuss the relevant projects they worked on.

Courses- I'll be honest, unless it's a relevant course for your profession, then most times you don't have to include it. College courses are up to you, but can be listed in the Education section.

Test Scores- More of a college student area than anything else, and as a recruiter, I have never looked at this area with any significance.

Organizations- This can be both professional and nonprofit. Show your commitment to the profession, especially if you hold a title position within a nationally recognized organization. This section provides information about professional development and involvement.

Causes- Briefly mention your interests, such as veterans, advocacy, or politics. As a recruiter, I've never really looked at this section myself.

Patents- Most do not have patents to list here, hence why it's only being briefly mentioned. List your patents here and take credit for the inventions you have created.

Languages- List out any languages you are fluent in, and I would also include this in your About section that you are bilingual, trilingual, etc.

CHAPTER 14

HOW TO ACTUALLY UTILIZE LINKEDIN

Do not tell or show my wife this, but I'm willing to bet my children's college fund that this will be the most-read chapter in the whole book. "How do you actually utilize LinkedIn effectively?" It is one of the top questions I am often asked during my presentations and mentorship sessions. I am going to break it down into four simple steps.

Step 1: It starts by creating a solid foundation with a fully optimized profile

Your profile is more than a digital rehash of your resume; it is the foundation of your online professional presence. Therefore, it must be detailed, personalized to you, and communicate that you are an expert in your field. At a minimum, you should have the books' chapter titles completed on your profile. This will allow you to achieve an optimized profile that will be search engine optimized and help you stand out to potential professional opportunities.

Step 2: Create content that is high quality, insightful, and relatable

This is probably the step that most users on LinkedIn struggle with. It is commonly stated that less than 1% of all LinkedIn users create content, while the other 99% are consumers of it. Typically, I have found that most professionals do not post because of one or a combination of the following issues, including imposter syndrome, fear of being wrong, being shy to "public speaking," or not having any idea of what to post. Here are some easy ideas for content creation: talk about your professional experience, share your opinion on industry trends, create memes related to your industry or relatable professional subjects, and provide insight into your industry that establishes that you are a Subject Matter Expert (SME).

When I first started on LinkedIn, I wasn't sure what to post and struggled with the same challenges I mentioned earlier. As a result, I initially shared content I felt comfortable with, which was memes. In a year and a half, it helped me steadily grow to a modest 15,000 following. I started analyzing profiles with more followers and engagement than mine. Based on these observations, I began experimenting with other types of content, such as videos, articles, and short-form posts. This approach has now helped me reach a respectable 26k+ followers and counting in just three years of being active on the platform. The screenshots below from LinkedIn Creator Analytics illustrate the relationship between content creation and visibility. I want you to think of your activity section like that of the feathers on a peacock. It allows you to stand out amongst the crowd, and on LinkedIn, that is a grand thing to achieve.

Analytics   Posts   Audience

Content performance ❓

1,261,566
Impressions

30k

20k

10k

0

Jul 23   Sep 21   Nov 20   Jan 19   Mar 20   May 19   Jul 18

Daily data is recorded in UTC

Nathanael, ex
with 1

Get the lat

About
Privacy
Advertis
Get U

Linked in

Discovery ❓

1,261,566   **307,171**
Impressions   Members reached

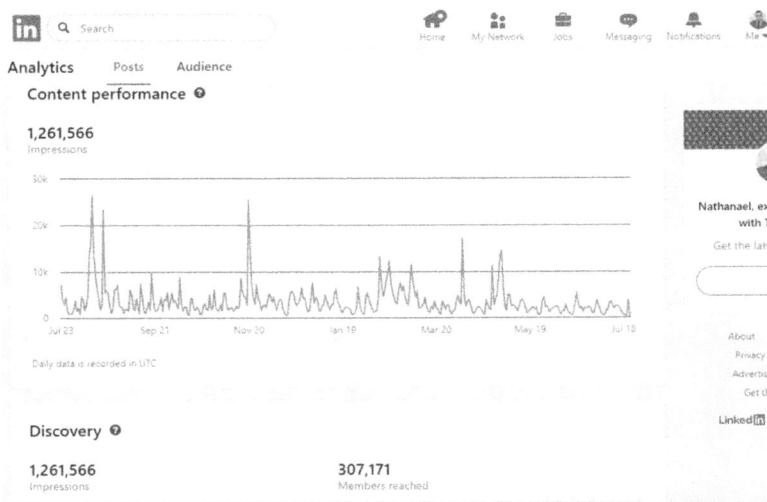

You can see from this image that even though I have around 26k followers, over 365 days of consistently posting content, my actual reach is 307,000+ members. Over 11 times greater than my actual follower count. LinkedIn tips state, "Members who post once a week can get up to 4x more profile views." Stay active!!!

Pro Tip: Use AI with content creation, brainstorming, and editing to help alleviate the stress of content creation.

Step 3: Build your presence through connections and followers

Start with your friends, family, coworkers, and classmates. This is your core network, both personally and professionally. You already have a real-life rapport. From there, you move to your expanded network by focusing on connecting with individuals in your professional field, field of interest, companies of interest, and recruitment professionals. These individuals are your door openers; they can open doors to knowledge, professional mentorship, and professional opportunities. If you have LinkedIn Creator mode on, then you can begin to develop followers, individuals who are not connected with you directly but enjoy your content/profile enough that they are following to see more of it in their timelines. Grow your audience organically or by actively engaging. LinkedIn allows users to send around 100 connection requests every seven days until you reach the maximum number of 30,000 connections. After that, you will not be able to send connection requests, but users who find your content/page interesting may select the option to follow your page, but will not be directly connected to you.

There is no ideal connection/follower count. It really depends on what you are trying to achieve on the platform that sets the goal post for your follower count.

Jobseekers- I found my first job with around 500 connections and my second role with around 15,000.

Businesses/Marketing- Obviously, the greater the follower count, the greater the opportunities for potential clients and brand marketing.

Recruitment professionals- Like businesses, I enjoy having a large following because that equals a greater potential candidate pool and reach for the roles I am recruiting.

Key Reminder- No matter what your follower count is, remember that they are people with their own wants and motivations. Try to do the next step as much as possible with your connections and followers to really maximize your network.

Step 4: Engage and network with other users

You would think that, because LinkedIn is a SOCIAL media site geared towards NETWORKING, that this would be obvious. Many users wrongly assume that offers will appear automatically once they create a profile. Unlike Indeed, you get to build content and actively engage with potential employers. Content functions as a conduit for user engagement by enabling informed and innovative individuals to produce material that others can interact with through comments, likes, and shares. From there, users can move or start conversations in the form of direct messages to each other's profiles. Request or offer mentorship, distribute resources, or make a referral. Even today, I still engage with my network through these means as well as by playing matchmaker.

Matchmaking is where I will introduce potential candidates to fellow recruiters in my network, free of charge. This helps all parties involved, and the goodwill I get in return is never a terrible thing. In fact, it was because of this very action that my current job approached me to speak about an opportunity on their TA team after a sizable number of my referrals ended up being placed there. My guiding philosophy is that I would want/hope someone would do it for me if/when I need it.

By following those simple four steps, you will see your engagement spike, your presence grow, and the opportunities start to flow in.

CHAPTER 15

MESSAGING DO'S & DON'TS

Messaging between users is essential for networking on LinkedIn. Like with all human communication, especially professionally, there are dos and don'ts to adhere to. Below are recommended guidelines for sending messages on LinkedIn, along with examples of practices to avoid.

Messaging Do's:

- **Personalize Your Message:** Refer to something specific about the recipient, such as their work, shared interests, or mutual connections.

- **Be Clear and Concise:** Keep your message brief, focused, and to the point. Respect their time.

- **Add Value:** Offer help, insights, or resources relevant to their industry or role.

- **Be professional:** Use polite and positive language.

- **Include a Call to Action:** Suggest next steps, like scheduling a call or meeting, politely.

- **Proofread:** Check for spelling and grammar mistakes to appear professional. Nothing ends a conversation before it starts like misspelling someone's name in an opening message.

- **Follow up:** If you don't get a response in 2-3 days, then send a follow-up message, as the recipient's inbox may be flooded with incoming messages, and yours got buried. This is a way to push your original message back up to the top. After two follow-up messages with no response, I would recommend moving on.

Messaging Don'ts:
- **Avoid Generic Messages:** Don't send overly salesy or mass messages; tailor each outreach.

- **Don't Be Pushy:** Respect their response time and avoid overly persistent follow-ups.

- **Don't Use Jargon or Slang:** Keep language professional and easy to understand.

- **Don't Ask for Too Much Too Soon:** Ideally, take time to build rapport before requesting favors or meetings.

- **Avoid Negative or Controversial Topics:** Keep your messaging positive and professional. LinkedIn is not a dating app!

Actual examples of bad messages from Jobseeker to Recruiter-

"Hi Nathaniel,

I'm interested in working at Leidos and saw that you work there. Please review my attached resume and let me know what roles best align with my skills.

Thank you, K."

****Recruiter perspective****

Starting off, they misspelled my name. Next, they listed the wrong organization. I work for Leidos QTC Health Services, not Leidos. Sending an unsolicited resume is the equivalent of sending unsolicited feet pics. 99% of the time, it doesn't lead to anything productive. It also shows that you are not taking the time to review our job board and instead expect the receiver to do the work for you. Instead, start by introducing yourself, the purpose of your message, and then, if the other party is interested, they'll ask for your resume.

Good example of a job seeker reaching out to a recruiter:

"Hi Nathanael,

My name is S.B., and I am an experienced software engineer interested in working for Leidos QTC Health Services. I checked your company's career website and found the position req number "SOFENG017335" that I believe I'm the ideal candidate for. I meet all the listed requirements, including 10+ years of experience, a bachelor's degree in software engineering, and an AWS practitioner certification. On top of that, my passion for helping the veteran community aligns with the organization's mission. If you agree with my assessment, I am happy to discuss further as well as send over my resume. Thank you, S.B."

Recruiter perspective

First, they spelled my name correctly and had the correct organization listed. They reviewed the organization, checked the career page, and found a suitable role that they wish to pursue. Listing the requisition number lets me review the role, find the recruiter, and discuss the position further with them to better advocate for you. This message directly addresses my questions.

CHAPTER 16

JOINING LINKEDIN GROUPS

LinkedIn groups are an underrated feature rarely mentioned by major users. These groups allow you to tap into a broader audience in your profession, discuss industry trends, and network. I recommend focusing on the Private groups over the Public because private groups are more selective about whom they let into the group. This allows for higher-quality discussions between professionals and keeps the spammers at bay. A group is only as good as its admins/moderators, as they are the ones controlling access to the group, moderating conversations, and encouraging engagement amongst the members.

Groups can be an excellent resource for job seekers as they are filled with potential mentors, resources, and possible employment opportunities. Many professional groups are set up by recruiters with the purpose of creating a private pool of candidates for sourcing opportunities. I'm guilty of it myself with the "Military Medical Professionals Network" both on LinkedIn and Facebook. It allows me the opportunity to balance altruism to help my fellow healthcare professionals and develop a talent pool to source from for my day job. I was inspired to do so after making the discovery that most of the social media groups that are for healthcare professionals are created/run by recruiters in those industries!!!

On the flip side, when I first made my transition into the recruitment field, the groups were the very first place I sought out. They provided me with the opportunity to immerse myself in the field by observing recruiters talk about their struggles, their wins, and most importantly, how they do it. This has enabled me to stay at the forefront of my field by keeping a finger on the pulse and exposure to rising trends. By the time of my first interview as a recruiter, I had a foundation of knowledge that allowed me to speak the lingo like I had been in the field for years. After I was hired, what I learned in the groups helped me avoid common pitfalls.

The groups also allowed me to substantially expand my professional network because of the networking events they hosted and the exposure to individuals that would typically be outside of my professional network. These connections have opened the door to knowledge, networking, research, and most importantly, mentorship. This mentorship and research have served as the catalyst for my own career.

Helpful tips for LinkedIn groups,

1. Focus on private groups for professional development and growth, while public groups open you up to more potential engagement.

2. Join groups in your profession, desired profession, or that you have a genuine interest in.

3. Engage proactively in group activities. As a group owner, always being the one to start the conversation is difficult, and then having zero engagement is disheartening. This is typically what you see in a sizable number of groups: people join, but no one starts the conversation. The whole point of these groups is to have conversations with professionals in your industry.

4. Network with individuals in the group, seek out or provide mentorship to members, and engage with their content.

CHAPTER 17

USING LINKEDIN KEY FEATURES

Utilize LinkedIn Creator mode to help grow your LinkedIn brand by utilizing and understanding key data analytics in the form of engagement, search appearances, followers, and profile views to refine your profile better.

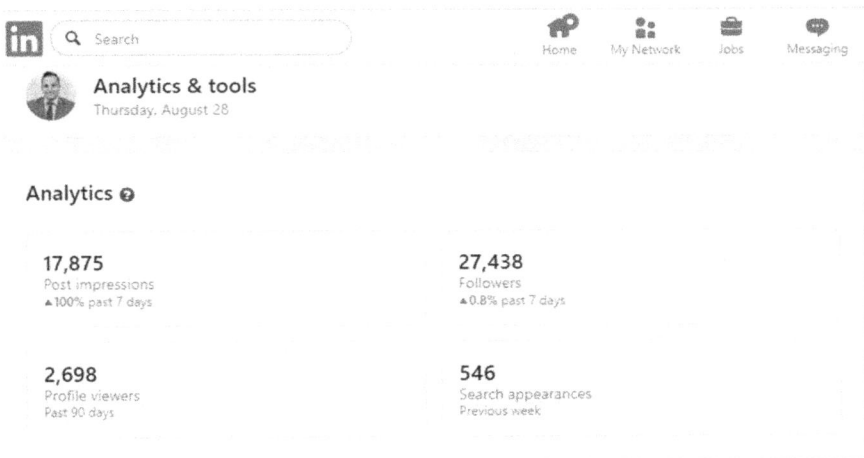

BREAKING DOWN ANALYTICS

Post Impressions — Impressions are the number of times your content is shown on someone's screen. Analyzing the number of impressions your post generates allows you to gain better insight into what is trending on the algorithm and platform itself. The greater the number, the greater visibility that post is generating for you. You can use this to identify ideal posting windows, types of content, and subject matter that are trending with your audience.

Profile Viewers- Seeing an increase in profile views means that your content is working and attracting individuals to view your profile. With premium, I like to track who is viewing my page, such as their employment status, titles, and industry. This provides me with insight into who my content is attracting to my page.

Followers- Are you gaining, losing, or maintaining followers throughout a given period? This lets you know if the content you are putting out is interesting enough to prompt individuals to follow you, or if you are being too controversial in your opinions on various subjects, potentially causing you to see a decrease in your follower count. Remember, your followers are your audience, and if you are looking to expand your sphere of influence on the platform, then you need to work on having a positive gain of followers weekly.

Search Appearances- Shows you how often your profile appeared across LinkedIn based on keyword search, posts, comments, and network recommendations. Obviously, the more frequently your profile appears, the higher your visibility and the higher your visibility, the more opportunities you will see on the platform.

APPLICATION OF ANALYTICS

As mentioned previously, utilize these key analytics to gain insight into your LinkedIn presence. Is your content gaining engagement, increasing your follower count, and profile views? If yes, then carry on, but if no, then you need to reevaluate your approach to continue optimizing your experience on the platform.

CHAPTER 18

HOW TO SPOT FAKE PROFILES & JOB SCAMS

As with any long-established social media platform with a large user base, the prevalence of scammers and fake profiles tends to increase over time. In this chapter, I'll analyze a recent follower to help you spot fake profiles.

First Red Flag — They are affiliated with a prominent, well-known brand and hold a highly influential position, such as an executive or work as a recruiter. Yet, they have zero to one followers or connections.

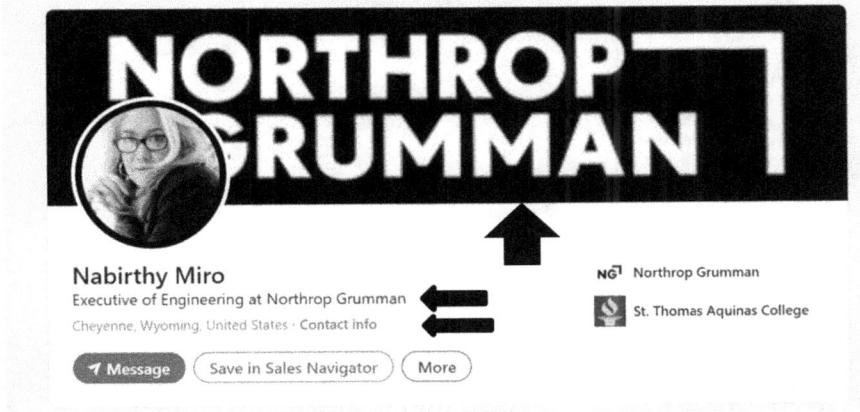

Second Red Flag- The profile was recently created within the past week for an individual with substantial experience. You can verify this by clicking the "More" button on a desktop profile or the three dots on a mobile device. Then, scroll to the bottom of the section and select "About this profile."

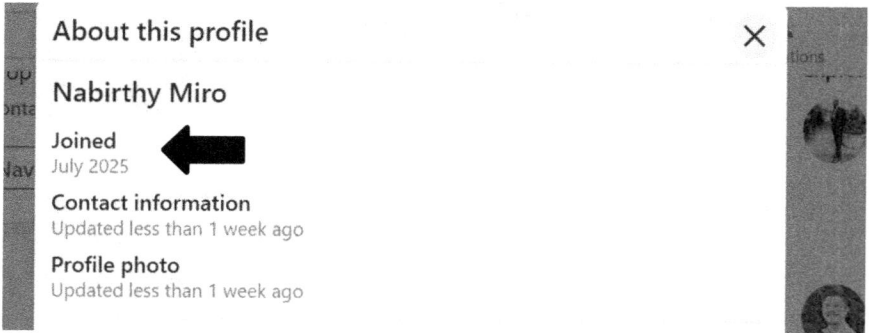

About this profile   ✕

Nabirthy Miro

Joined
July 2025

Contact information
Updated less than 1 week ago

Profile photo
Updated less than 1 week ago

Third Red Flag- Under the "Posts" section in Activity, there are only reposts with no original content, and the profile has zero followers.

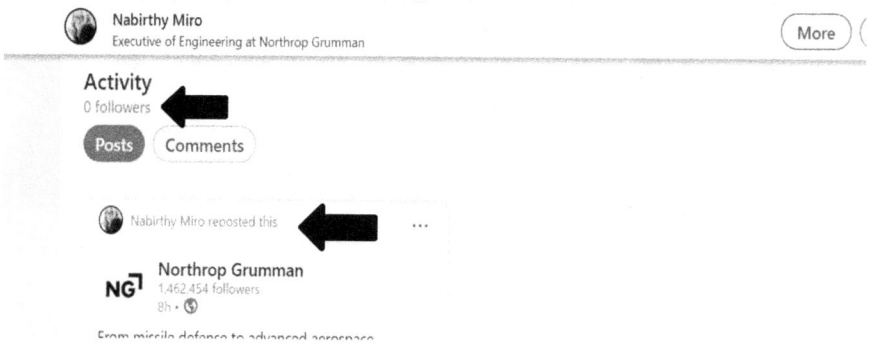

Nabirthy Miro
Executive of Engineering at Northrop Grumman   More

Activity
0 followers

Posts   Comments

Nabirthy Miro reposted this   ...

NG Northrop Grumman
1,462,454 followers
8h · 🌐

From missile defense to advanced aerospace

Fourth Red Flag - The Comments section in Activity is filled with identical spam comments, which are unsolicited and irrelevant to the posts they are replying to, where the original poster is not seeking work or related content.

Comments usually ask individuals to send their resume to a colleague or directly to the recruiter, typically using a @gmail.com email address. Most major organizations use their own domain emails, so this is unusual. A quick Google search can confirm that this is the incorrect format for the organization. For example, the legitimate Northrop Grumman email format would be Firstname.Lastname@NGC.com.

Nabirthy Miro · 3rd+   3h ···
Executive of Engineering at Northrop Grumman

JR Ewing, Not every job makes it to the job boards, some go straight to
the top candidates.
This is one of those chances.

Nina at Northrop Grumman is hiring for remote and on-site roles across
multiple industries and these openings haven't been posted yet. Based
on your background, you could be a great match.

If you're open to new opportunities, reach out to her
directly: nina.llove.ng@northropgrummanusa.com ◀━━
Send your resume and a quick note about what you're looking for.

She's reviewing candidates this week don't miss out.

Like | Reply

Add a reply...   ☺   🖼

Fifth Red Flag — The profile has illogical inconsistencies, such
as conflicting experience details. For example, in the Northrop
Grumman Experience section, they appear to have mistakenly
included their Verizon job experience in the wrong location.

Sixth Red Flag – If an internal recruiter asks for payment or recommends their contact to review your resume, it's a clear signal of fraud.

What to do next?

If you come across one of these profiles, please act as a responsible LinkedIn user and report the profile as "not a real person." This enables LinkedIn to more efficiently detect and eliminate fraudulent accounts, thereby safeguarding its community. Your efforts can prevent other users from falling victim to these deceptive frauds.

CHAPTER 19

BUILDING YOUR NETWORK WITH AN OMNI-CHANNEL APPROACH

In an earlier chapter, I mentioned the importance of balancing your network with quantity and quality connections rather than just focusing on connecting with everyone. This chapter will be the exception to that rule, and it's more geared to those who are trying to be a professional influencer. These individuals are planning to use this large, established network as a resource either to market a product or service to their audience or to use this established network as part of their value proposition to potential employers. Take me, for example. The reason I want to continue to grow my network as large as possible is that, as a recruiter, my greatest asset is my access to a large pool of qualified candidates that other recruiters may not have access to.

Look at any of the major influencers with a large following, and you can see there is a critical element to all their success. The main factor is building a broad network through an omnichannel strategy. An omnichannel approach for social media influencers involves strategically using multiple platforms to create a seamless and consistent brand experience for your audience. Instead of just focusing on one platform like LinkedIn, an omnichannel approach integrates content across various channels such as YouTube, TikTok, Facebook, email, newsletters, and even a brand's website. This approach aims to maximize reach, boost brand recall, and drive conversions by meeting the audience where they are and providing a consistent brand experience.

To build your LinkedIn channel specifically, use the other channels to pipeline potential followers to your profile. So, at the end of every video or content you generate, you want to have a call to action and invite them to follow your profile. This allows you to continuously convert traffic into followers you might not have been able to engage with on LinkedIn alone.

Understand that the content strategy that works for one channel may not work for another. For example, meaningful posts or short-form videos do well on LinkedIn, but on YouTube, long-form videos are the way to go. Although the format of your content may vary across different channels, it is vital to ensure that your brand message stays consistent. I always encourage my clients to be adaptable to their content but consistent in their branding message. This helps you avoid confusing your audience, where on one platform you are ultra conservative, and on the other, you are a troll.

CHAPTER 20

LINKEDIN LEARNING

Many LinkedIn users overlook LinkedIn Learning. It is an online platform offering video courses taught by industry experts on a wide range of professional topics, including business, artificial intelligence, and certification training. It's an excellent resource to continue your professional development.

Courses and certifications offer a way to show knowledge and add credentials to a resume. Upon starting my career in recruitment, I used LinkedIn Learning to efficiently gain industry-specific knowledge, terminology, practical strategies, and compliance requirements relevant to the field. This helped with my learning curve as I made a successful career pivot into a new role.

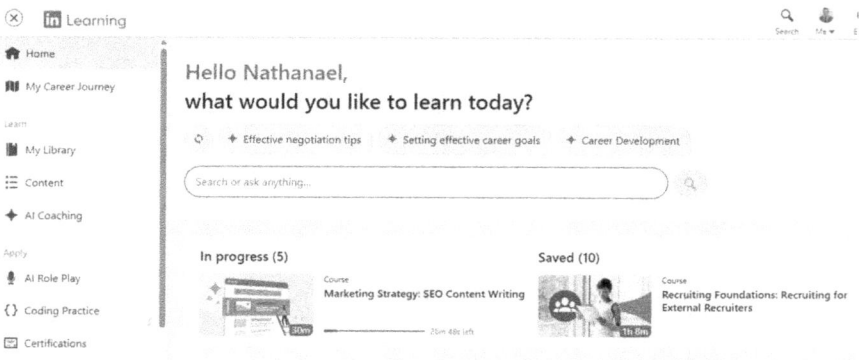

Recruiter Perspectives

For me, when I see that a candidate has recent courses, it lets me know that they are continuing to develop themselves and that they are staying up to date on changing industry trends. Professional certifications from name brands go a long way to legitimizing what you bring to the table and help tip the scales in your favor as you are going through the hiring process. Certifications offer more up-to-date, specialized knowledge than most degrees and are typically more affordable.

When work is slow or you are looking to make a career pivot, LinkedIn Learning is an excellent way to build foundational knowledge in your new industry, stay up to date on industry trends, and more.

CHAPTER 21

LINKEDIN PREMIUM

There are two versions of Premium, one for business and the other for individuals. This chapter will be focused on the individual plan meant for job seekers. By upgrading to Premium, you unlock a plethora of unique features such as an AI assistant, advanced search filters, and more that we will cover throughout this chapter.

Quick stats directly pulled from LinkedIn's website illustrate the impact on users who upgrade to Premium.

- "Premium subscribers who've applied to LinkedIn job posts using Top choice jobs are on average **43% more likely to receive a message back from a recruiter**."

- "Premium members are **39% more likely to hear back after applying for a job** on LinkedIn."

- "Applicants who sent InMails to job posters were **1.6x more likely to hear back and 3x more likely to get hired**."

- "Premium members are **2.6x more likely to get hired** on average on LinkedIn."

As you can see, upgrading to Premium can have a significant impact on your overall LinkedIn experience, but mainly as a job seeker. While a conclusive list of all the advanced features of Premium is available on the LinkedIn website, I will be focusing on the ones that I feel, as a recruiter, have the most significant impact.

Premium Features:

1. Advance Search Filters- "Filter for people who are actively hiring, and jobs where you are a top applicant." This can significantly reduce your search time by zeroing in on the users who are actively hiring for roles.

2. Who's viewed your profile- "See a list of viewers, trends, and insights for the past 365 days. Browse profiles anonymously." As a recruiter, this is one of my favorite features with Premium because it provides me with insights into who my profile is attracting. *Pro Tip* If someone looks at your profile and you are interested in what they potentially have to offer, then I highly recommend connecting with them or using one of your InMails. Seeing that they viewed your profile tells you that they are an active profile and that they are interested in you. If you don't receive a message, don't be discouraged; many people, including recruiters, may hesitate to reach out first. Take the leap and message them first. It shows initiative and helps build upon the interest they already have in your profile.

3. InMail- Allows you to message an individual outside of your network. With Premium, you get 5 of these a month, so be strategic with them. Target individuals who are actively hiring for roles that you are interested in and are qualified for.

4. Access to LinkedIn Learning- One of the lesser-used features by most users is LinkedIn Learning. Whenever I teach an optimization course, I'm always shocked by how little people use this fantastic feature. You get access to

24k+ courses that can help you either set up a solid foundation in a subject or further refine the knowledge you have by attending classes taught by subject matter experts.

5. AI assistant- 2025 is the year of AI, and it can be seen with LinkedIn increasing its implementation of AI to aid job seekers. AI can provide insight on job postings, aid you with writing content or drafting messages, and it can even provide coaching for you through LinkedIn Learning. AI can be a game-changer in enhancing your efficiency on the platform.

Upgrading to a LinkedIn Premium account can offer benefits to job seekers across different seniority levels and fields. It only works if you actively use the advanced features being provided to you. If you just create a profile and never use it, then you are quite literally throwing money away.

Recruiter Perspective

For all the job seekers struggling with the decision of whether to upgrade their account or not....do it. It's incredibly beneficial, especially with it unlocking a plethora of features that increase your efficiency on the platform. Think of it as a small investment for yourself and increasing your future wages.

CHAPTER 22

LINKEDIN RECRUITER

You could think of LinkedIn Recruiter as the premium version of LinkedIn for talent acquisition specialists, as premium is to regular job seekers. LinkedIn Recruiter is LinkedIn's premier talent acquisition platform that is designed to help organizations streamline their end-to-end hiring process. It leverages real-time insights, AI-driven advanced search filters, automated candidate matching, and messaging tools to give users the full experience of recruiting on LinkedIn. I do want to clarify that not every recruiter on LinkedIn is utilizing LinkedIn Recruiter to source their candidates primarily due to its hefty price tag of almost $10k annually per seat! Another key thing to note is that when you are going to put on your green banner, and LinkedIn asks if you want to make it available to recruiters only, this is who they mean. Hence, it severely limits your visibility on the platform if you choose this option vs if you choose the general one.

When you say LinkedIn Recruiter, there are really two options. There is LinkedIn Recruiter Lite, which has more limited features and costs around $200 a month, or LinkedIn Recruiter, which is the complete suite offering. This chapter will focus on LinkedIn Recruiter, as everything discussed will also encompass LinkedIn Recruiter Lite.

Key Features-

1. Expanded Network Access

- **Total Network Search:** Unlike Lite, which limits your search to 1st, 2nd, and 3rd-degree connections, the full Recruiter seat allows you to search and view the entire LinkedIn network of 1B+ members, even those completely outside your personal network.

- **No "Private Profile" Walls:** You won't see the "LinkedIn Member" placeholder; you get complete profile visibility for everyone on the platform.

2. Advanced AI & Search Filters

While Lite has roughly 20 filters, the full version offers 40+ filters, including:

- **"Open to Work" (Private):** View candidates who have privately signaled to recruiters they are looking for jobs (without their current employer knowing). This is what I mentioned previously as the alternative option to listing your "open to work" banner for the general public.

- **Relocation Filter:** Find candidates who have explicitly indicated they are open to moving to your specific city.

- **Skill Assessments:** Filter for candidates who have verified their skills through LinkedIn's official tests.

- **Advanced Experience Filters:** Search by "Years in Current Role," "Years in Current Company," and "Company Size" history.

3. **High-Volume Outreach**
   - **150 InMails per month:** If candidates "accept" or "decline," you will receive credit back, and InMails allow you to move straight to the top of the inbox and stand out there.

   - **Bulk Messaging:** Send personalized InMails to up to **25 candidates at once** using templates.

   - **Smart InMail:** AI-assisted messaging that drafts personalized outreach based on the candidate's profile and your job description.

4. **Enterprise Collaboration & Workflow**
   - **Multi-User Projects:** Share candidate folders (Projects) with your entire team. You can see your teammates' notes, tags, and whether they have already messaged a candidate to avoid "double-tapping." This helps when you are establishing and maintaining multiple candidate pipelines for current and future opportunities.

   - **Collaborator Seats:** You can provide free "Collaborator" seats to Hiring Managers so they can review your shortlisted candidates and leave feedback directly in the platform.

   - **ATS Integration (RSC):** The "Recruiter System Connect" feature allows you to sync LinkedIn with your Applicant Tracking System (like Greenhouse, Lever, or Workday). You can see if a candidate is already in your database without leaving LinkedIn.

5. **Advanced Analytics & Reporting**
   - **Pipeline Analytics:** Detailed reports on your hiring funnel, showing where candidates are dropping off.

- **InMail Performance:** Track response rates across your team to see which templates are most effective.

- **Diversity Insights:** Real-time data to help you understand the gender and location diversity of your talent pool.

Recruiter Perspective

As a recruiter, all these features are force multipliers to increase your efficiency in sourcing and recruiting potential candidates significantly. It helps us cut hours from our sourcing time and cut through a lot of the "dead" profiles on LinkedIn that we would otherwise take valuable time screening or messaging for no response. For job seekers, understanding the LinkedIn Recruiter and especially the filters it utilizes will help you further optimize your presence on the platform.

CHAPTER 23

FINAL THOUGHTS

"Knowledge is only potential power. It becomes power only when, and if, it is organized into definite plans of action, and directed to a definite end." (Napoleon Hill, Think and Grow Rich: The Original 1937 Unedited Edition) The reason I put that quote as the first sentence of my final chapter is that I want it to serve as a call to action for you. Reading this book is only half the battle; the other half is implementing it on your LinkedIn profile. If you just read this book and do nothing, then you wasted your money on this purchase. The knowledge in this book is meant to be applied, not memorized, like some textbook in school.

I guarantee that once you start applying the knowledge of this book on your page, you are going to see your presence begin to grow on the platform. After that, as mentioned before, it's about remaining consistent and staying up to date. Some of the information in this book's relevance will change as the platform's algorithm continues to change with the shifts of audiences' attention. However, two things that will always remain essential to any LinkedIn strategy are having a fleshed-out profile and consistent online activity.

Look forward to seeing you achieve success on the platform and all your future endeavors, and thank you for your support in my endeavor with the writing of this book. Remember to send me a request, and let's connect.

BIBLIOGRAPHY

LinkedIn Timeline-
https://www.nytimes.com/2016/06/14/technology/a-linkedin-timeline.html

LinkedIn Timeline-
https://about.linkedin.com/

LinkedIn Company Information- LinkedIn. (n.d.). About LinkedIn. Retrieved July 21, 2025, from
https://about.linkedin.com/

LinkedIn Demographics-
https://www.linkedhelper.com/blog/linkedin-demographics/

LinkedIn Demographics-
https://www.sprinklr.com/blog/linkedin-demographics/

LinkedIn Profile Picture Stats-
https://www.linkedin.com/business/sales/blog/b2b-sales/picture-perfect--make-a-great-first-impression-with-your-linkedi

Imposter Syndrome Definition-
https://www.merriam-webster.com/dictionary/impostor%20syndrome

LinkedIn Articles-
https://www.linkedin.com/advice/3/what-ideal-length-blog-post-skills-content-creation-guz6e

Boolean Search Strings- *LibGuides: Database Search Tips: Boolean operators*. **(n.d.).**
https://libguides.mit.edu/c.php?g=175963&p=1158594)

LinkedIn Premium-
https://premium.linkedin.com/

LinkedIn Sales Navigator-
https://business.linkedin.com/sales-solutions/sales-navigator/b?adobe_mc_sdid=SDID%3D11D425C225F75D82-3297BFCAA6F5BDC6%7CMCORGID%3D14215E3D5995C57C0A495C55%40AdobeOrg%7CTS%3D1753555418&adobe_mc_ref=https%3A%2F%2Fwww.google.com%2F

LinkedIn Recruiter-
https://business.linkedin.com/talent-solutions/recruiter